THE ADVENTURES OF EDDIE & EMMA EYEBALL

Written, produced,
& Created By:
Simrun Kalra

Illustrations by:
Somesh Kumar

copyright©2008

FOR MY LOVING FATHER, WHO ENCOURAGED ME WHEN I HAD DOUBTS, PRAISED ME WHEN I SHINED, AND RE- MINDED ME OF HOW MUCH BETTER I COULD DO WHEN I STUMBLED. FOR MY MOTHER WHOSE KINDNESS FILLS ME, AND FOR MY BROTHER WHOSE GRACE INSPIRES ME.

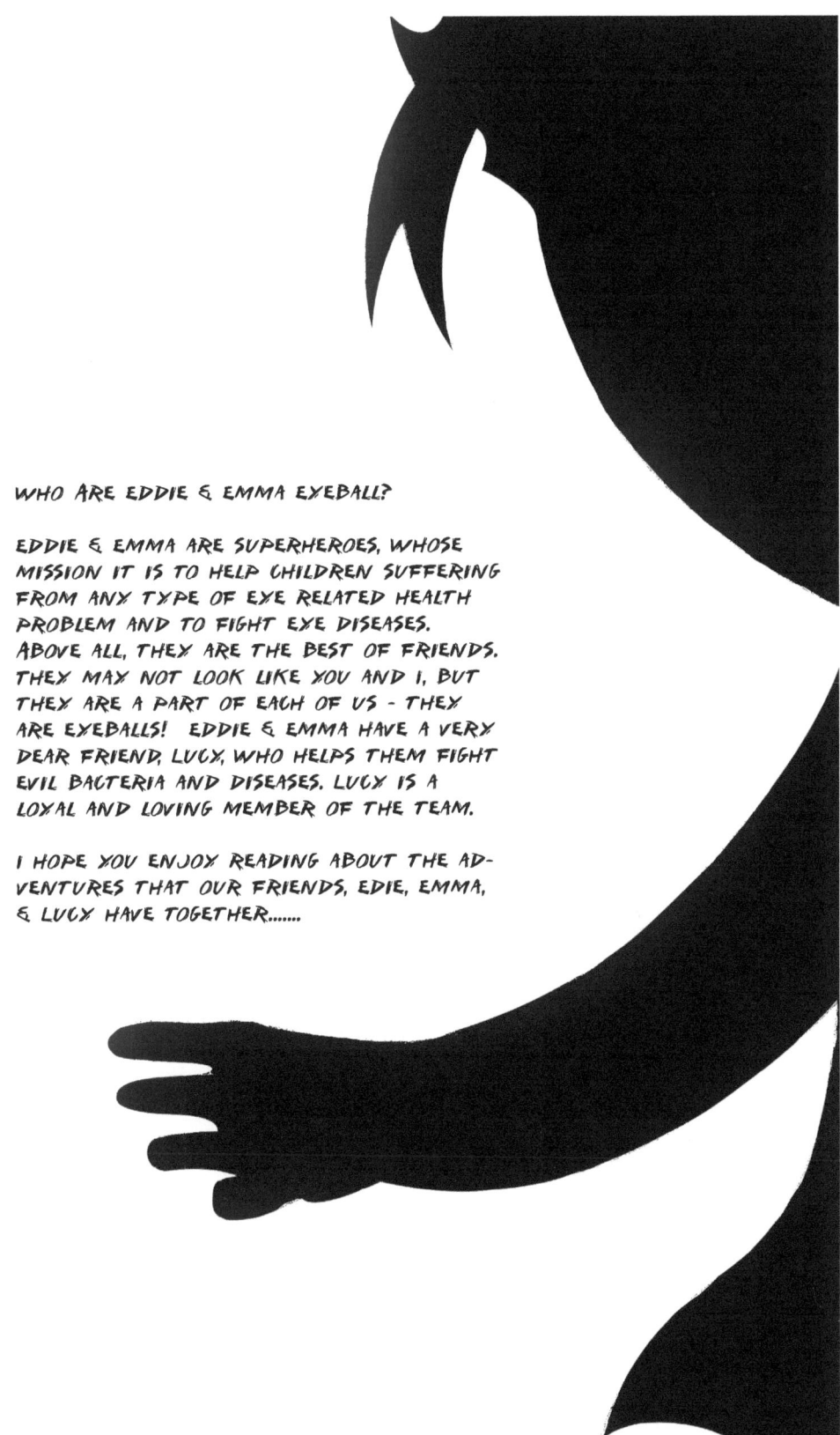

WHO ARE EDDIE & EMMA EYEBALL?

EDDIE & EMMA ARE SUPERHEROES, WHOSE MISSION IT IS TO HELP CHILDREN SUFFERING FROM ANY TYPE OF EYE RELATED HEALTH PROBLEM AND TO FIGHT EYE DISEASES. ABOVE ALL, THEY ARE THE BEST OF FRIENDS. THEY MAY NOT LOOK LIKE YOU AND I, BUT THEY ARE A PART OF EACH OF US - THEY ARE EYEBALLS! EDDIE & EMMA HAVE A VERY DEAR FRIEND, LUCY, WHO HELPS THEM FIGHT EVIL BACTERIA AND DISEASES. LUCY IS A LOYAL AND LOVING MEMBER OF THE TEAM.

I HOPE YOU ENJOY READING ABOUT THE ADVENTURES THAT OUR FRIENDS, EDIE, EMMA, & LUCY HAVE TOGETHER.......

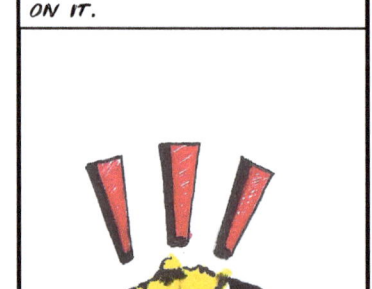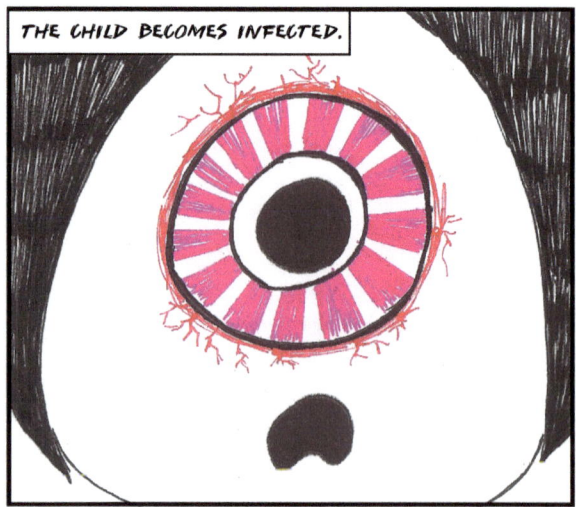

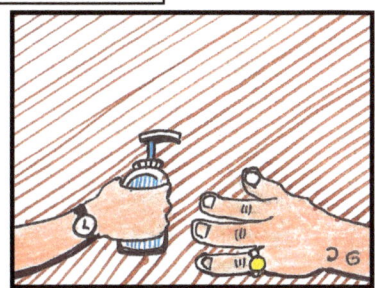

THE WHOLE SHOP IS NOW IN CHAOS WITH PINK EYES AND REGULAR EYEBALLS GOING AT IT.

SOME RUN FOR THE DOOR. AT THE END OF THE BATTLE, ALL OF THE PINK EYES ARE EITHER DEAD OR RAN AWAY. EDDIE, EMMA, THE CHAI WALLAH AND A FEW REGULARS SPREAD OUT AROUND THE PLACE TRY TO CATCH THEIR BREATH AS THEY SURVEY WHAT'S LEFT.

WELL EDDIE, NOW WE KNOW THE SECRET TO FIGHTING CONJUNCTIVITIS AND HIS GANG OF PINK EYES AND WE HAVE TO SHARE IT WITH EVERYONE. WE CAN GET SOME MEDICINE FOR EVERYONE THAT'S ALREADY BEEN INFECTED AND MAKE SURE WE SPREAD THE WORD TO EVERYONE ON HOW TO FIGHT CONJUNCTIVITIS AND HIS GANG SO THAT THEY NEVER COME BACK.

A JOB WELL DONE EMMA, IF I DO SAY SO MYSELF. NOW LET'S GO GET SOME SCHOOL CHILDREN - AND THEIR PARENTS NO DOUBT - SOME MUCH NEEDED RELIEF!

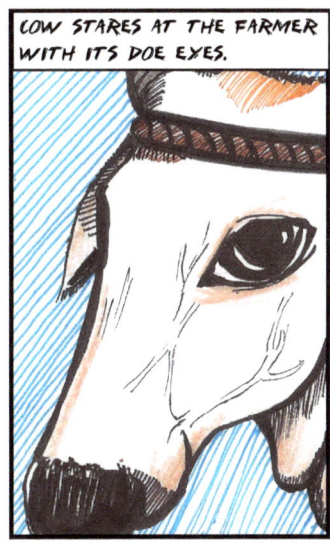

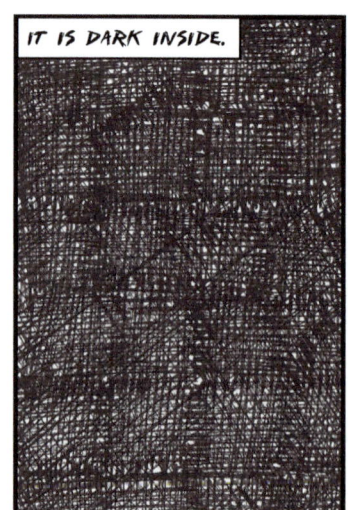

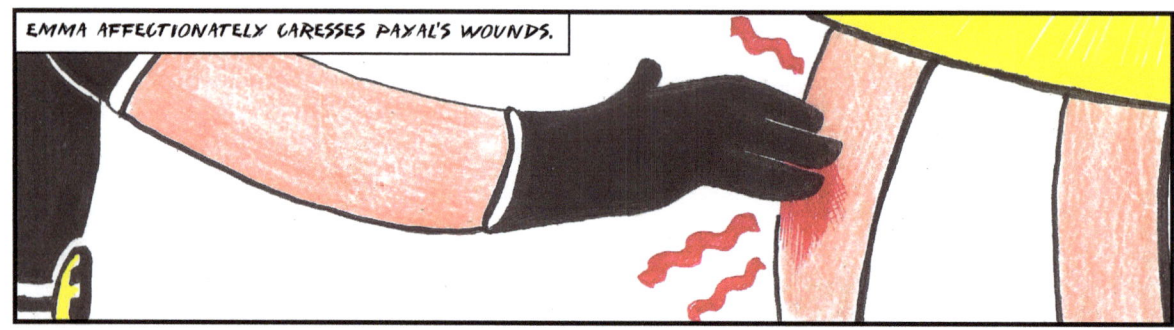

ALL OF THESE THINGS,

THE BITOT SPOTS, DRYNESS OF THE EYES, POOR VISION AT NIGHT

ARE CAUSED BY **VITAMIN A** DEFICIENCY.

IT IS COMMON IN CHILDREN BETWEEN THE AGES OF

6 MONTHS, 6 YEARS, PREGNANT WOMEN AND WOMEN WHO ARE LACTATING

"IN FACT, I AM WONDERING IF THE REASON PAYAL FELL AND COULDN'T SEE THE PILE OF WOOD IN THE TOOL SHED YESTERDAY IS BECAUSE SHE IS ALSO LACKING ENOUGH VITAMIN A."

"WHY WOULD WE NOT HAVE ENOUGH VITAMIN A? THIS HASN'T BEEN A PROBLEM BEFORE."

"HAS YOUR DIET CHANGED RECENTLY?"

"WELL YES, WITH THE DROUGHT, WE HAVEN'T HAD MUCH OF A HARVEST AT ALL AND FOOD HAS BEEN SCARCE IN GENERAL. WE EAT WHAT LITTLE RICE THERE IS LEFT AND OCCASIONALLY SOME ONION OR POTATOES. SOON, EVEN THE RICE WILL RUN OUT."

"NO PROBLEM! I'M ON IT."

"LUCY? WE NEED YOU HELP! ALL OF THE CHILDREN IN THE VILLAGE AND NEW MOTHERS NEED TO BE SCREENED FOR VITAMIN A DEFICIENCY AND WE'LL NEED A LOT OF VITAMIN A SUPPLEMENTS FOR THOSE THAT SCREEN POSITIVE FOR THE DEFICIENCY."

THE NEXT DAY WE SEE LUCY HEADING UP THE EFFORT TO GATHER PEOPLE INTO AN ORGANIZED FASHION TO BE SCREENED BY THE QUALIFIED VOLUNTEERS SHE HAS RECRUITED.

CLINIC

PLEASE KEEP SILENCE

PATIENTS

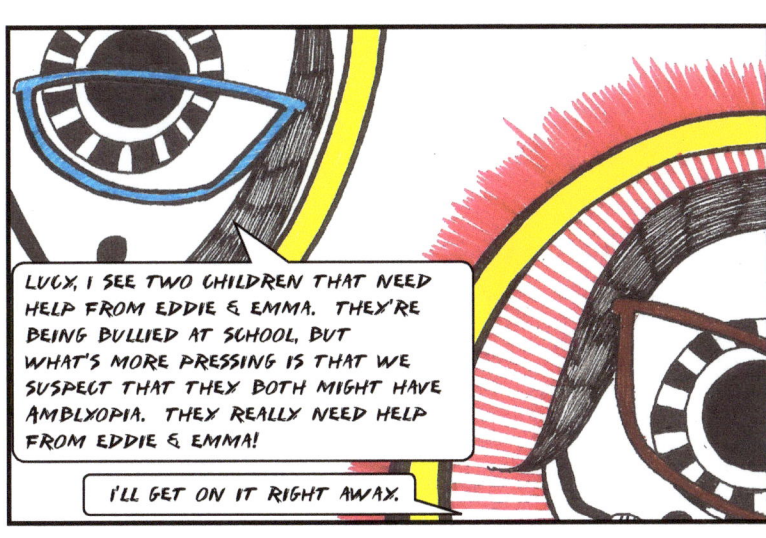

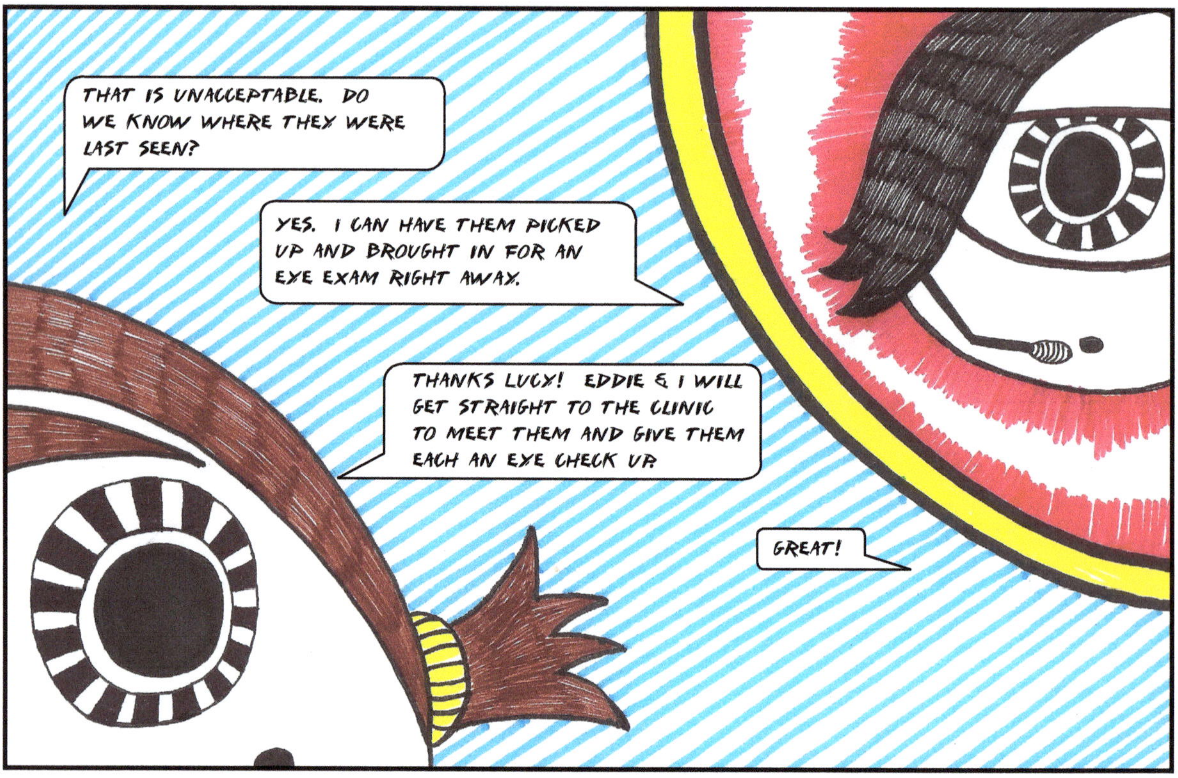

Panel 1:

"THAT IS UNACCEPTABLE. DO WE KNOW WHERE THEY WERE LAST SEEN?"

"YES. I CAN HAVE THEM PICKED UP AND BROUGHT IN FOR AN EYE EXAM RIGHT AWAY."

"THANKS LUCY! EDDIE & I WILL GET STRAIGHT TO THE CLINIC TO MEET THEM AND GIVE THEM EACH AN EYE CHECK UP."

"GREAT!"

Panel 2:

AT THE CLINIC......

"WELL, IF THEY HAVE AMBLYOPIA WE WILL KNOW BECAUSE ONE EYE WILL BE MUCH STRONGER THAN THE OTHER ONE."

"THAT'S RIGHT, AND THEY MIGHT BE SUFFERING FROM EYE STRAIN, HEADACHES, AND HAVE TO SQUINT OR CLOSE ONE EYE IN ORDER TO SEE."

"I CAN IMAGINE HOW PEOPLE MIGHT BE TEASING THEM. WE SHOULD HELP SOME OF THOSE CHILDREN REMEMBER THAT IT ISN'T RIGHT TO MAKE FUN OF SOMEONE JUST BECAUSE THEY ARE DIFFERENT."

www.ingramcontent.com/pod-product-compliance
Lightning Source LLC
Chambersburg PA
CBHW041226040426
42444CB00002B/63